# PUPPIES
## by
## Wendy Boorer

## Hamlyn
## London·New York·Sydney·Toronto

# CONTENTS

First Published 1970
Second Impression 1971

Published by the Hamlyn Publishing Group Limited
London · New York · Sydney · Toronto
Hamlyn House, Feltham, Middlesex, England
© The Hamlyn Publishing Group Limited, 1970
Printed in Canary Islands (Spain) by
Litografia A. Romero, S.A., Santa Cruz de Tenerife
ISBN 0 600 34813 X

# INTRODUCTION

Puppies, like all baby animals, need a great deal of sleep.

There is no animal in the world that has formed so close an association with man as the dog. The partnership could have started as long as ten thousand years ago, when man was still a hunter, wandering in small groups in search of food. Three or four thousand years later man had started to tame and domesticate other animals and needed dogs to guard and drive his flocks and herds.

From this beginning, when man began to breed different kinds of dogs for different jobs, springs the hundreds of breeds that we can find in the world today. This book shows you some of them when they are young and tells you how they grow up and develop. It helps you to choose between them, and to care for them and train them—for the partnership which started so long ago is still a flourishing one, even though today a dog's role is less hunter and guard than simply man's best friend.

# WILD DOGS

The dog's wild relatives are a group of animals which include Wolves, Foxes and Jackals. Members of this wild dog family are found all over the world. Some live in the extreme cold of the Arctic regions. Others survive in hot, desert areas, or roam in packs through bush country. Still others live in the jungles of the tropics. Because different members of this wild dog family live and breed successfully in such widely different climates and surroundings, they are, unlike many families of animals, in no danger yet of dying out.

This puppy looks like any fireside pet but it is in fact a young Australian Dingo. Dingo puppies, if caught young enough, can be tamed, but even those reared by humans cannot be trusted always to remain friendly when adult.

A cuddly Coyote puppy like this would turn into a spitting, snarling bundle of fury if approached too closely by a man. This inherited fear of humans is one of the things that distinguishes wild dogs from pet dogs.

8

The African or Cape Hunting-dog has a blotched irregular coat which may be useful for camouflage. Packs of these animals are widely feared because of their savagery.

All Wolves, Foxes and Jackals are carnivorous. This means that they are hunting animals eating mainly meat. To hunt successfully they must first find their prey and this is where their keen sense of smell and their acute hearing are of invaluable help. To catch and kill their food, they must be able to run fast and be equipped with powerful jaw muscles and strong teeth. Most of the dog's nearest relatives live in packs, the members of which help each other in the hunting and killing of game. This co-operation between members of a group is one of the things that dogs have inherited from their wild ancestors.

The Wolf is one of the dog's nearest relatives and some people believe that all dogs are descended from wolf-like ancestors. Wolves and dogs can breed together, and Wolf cubs can be tamed fairly easily. But Wolf cubs born from tame parents are still wild and have to be tamed in their turn. A fully grown Wolf can be as much as thirty-one inches at the shoulder and weigh over a hundred pounds, so they are both larger and stronger than the average dog.

Wolves used to be found throughout most of Europe and North America, but man has exterminated them from many areas and they are now only found in the Arctic and northern tundras. A pair of Wolves will stay together for life, rearing a litter of cubs in the spring and summer, if the supply of food is plentiful. While the mother is caring for the cubs, which are usually born in an underground den, the male Wolf hunts and brings home food for his family. When the cubs are old enough to be left for short periods, both parents go out hunting to bring food back. In the autumn and winter both adults and the litter hunt together. This small group of five or six, often with a lone male or odd single female attached, is the usual Wolf pack.

The African Hunting-dog is not closely related to the dog, having, among other differences, four toes on their front feet rather than five as in the dog and Wolf. They are even more social in their habits, living in packs of up to fifty. All members of the pack work together in hunting, caring for and feeding the cubs.

The Coyote is an animal found in North and Central America and is often known as the Prairie Wolf. It is smaller than the more northern Timber Wolf, being only about twenty-four inches at the shoulder and weighing forty pounds. They are more solitary in their habits than either Wolves or Hunting-dogs, but do combine in groups to catch larger game such as deer. They are very adaptable animals, and when the country where they live is changed by farming and agriculture, the Coyote will vary its diet and hunting methods in order to continue living there. For this reason, even though men have tried to kill them off, Coyotes are still quite widespread.

These Wolf cubs are just getting to the stage when they want to explore their surroundings.

A Fox cub, hand-reared from a young age, plays happily with a litter of Beagles.

10

In Europe the only member of the wild dog family which is at all common is the Red Fox. The Foxes form a group on their own and are not close relatives of the dog. The Red Fox is a solitary animal with rather cat-like hunting methods. It relies on the stealthy approach and the quick pounce, rather than exhausting its prey by a long chase. An animal that includes poultry and lambs in its diet, the Red Fox, is an enemy of the farmer, who does his best to rid his land of them. The Fox survives because it is wary and cunning, and hunts mostly at night. Red Foxes, too, are adaptable. They used to feed mainly on rabbits, but when most of these died out, Red Foxes took to feeding on small rodents like mice and voles. They have even been known to search dustbins and make garbage part of their diet.

The Dingo is now a wild dog but it is thought that, in the past, Dingos were once completely domesticated. Dingos are found in Australia and are believed to have been brought there by the first Aborigines to reach that continent. This was many thousands of years ago, and the Dingo, finding food plentiful, deserted man and went back to the wild.

Wild dogs have their litters of cubs during the spring. Not only is the weather warmer then but the food supply is more abundant and hunting is easier. Caring for the litter of cubs occupies nearly all the mother's time for the first two or three weeks and she has to rely very often on the male animal bringing food back to the den. If he had to roam too far in making a kill, hunger could, it is true, force the mother to desert her litter. In spring, however, there are always plenty of other young animals around for a wild dog to catch and feed to his own mate and offspring.

The sweet and gentle expression on the face of this tri-colour Shetland Sheepdog shows clearly the charms of the Collie in miniature. Though they may be aloof with strangers, Shelties are affectionate and loving towards their owners.

Siberian Huskies very often have blue eyes.

# A PUPPY'S EARLY LIFE

When a domestic bitch has her young she shows many similarities in behaviour to her wild relatives. Left to herself, she would seek a safe secluded den. There are many instances of pet dogs digging their own burrows before giving birth to their litters. Farm dogs will often tunnel into haystacks and create a warm, cosy nest that way. Most owners prefer their pets to have a litter of puppies in a kennel or outhouse, or a room which can be set aside for the purpose. The best kind of bed for the mother and puppies is some kind of box. The top must be removable so that, should anything go wrong, the animals can be looked at and easily reached. The door to the box should be just large enough for the mother to get through and the whole thing should be raised an inch or so from the floor as a protection against draughts. The enclosed space inside such a box satisfies the bitch's need for seclusion, quiet and darkness, all of which spell safety to the instincts she has inherited from her wild ancestors. The size of the box depends very greatly on the size of the breed of dog, but it should be high enough for the mother to be able to stand up comfortably, and the floor area should allow her ample room to stretch out flat on her side. An added refinement would be a guard rail running round the inside of the box, an inch or so away from the side and two or three inches above the floor. This can prevent a very young puppy from getting squashed or smothered by a rather clumsy mother.

The best bedding for a mother and new born puppies is newspaper, because it is cheap and can be changed two or three times a day as soon as it becomes wet and smelly. Many bitches

Welsh Springer Spaniels are one of the Gundog breeds. Most of the Gundogs like human companionship and are easy to train. The Spaniel's job was to find game for the sportsman to shoot, and Spaniels were expected to search for and bring back the dead birds. For this reason it is often quite easy to teach these dogs to fetch and carry things in their mouths.
Welsh Springer Spaniels are not as well known as some of the other Spaniel breeds. They may be recognised by their rich, dark red and white colouring.

At nine days old puppies are still blind.

scratch and dig for hours, and sometimes days, before their puppies are due to be born, and this, too, is a relic from the past when the wild dog started preparing a den for the cubs about to be born.

In other respects though, dogs differ from Wolves. The father has no part in bringing up the puppies. Should he be allowed near when the puppies are very small, the mother herself will drive him away. When they are three weeks old or so, the mother may allow him near but will usually remain and keep a wary eye on the situation. In fact most male dogs will tolerate puppies quite well but often look comically embarrassed when their paws and tail are seized on as playthings. They seem to feel this is a slight to their dignity and will make their escape as quickly as they can. For many thousands of years the dog has depended on man for its food, and there is no need for the male to go out hunting for his offspring.

Another effect of domestication is that pet dogs can have their litters at any time of the year, and not just in the spring when so many of the wild animals are born. The number of puppies in a litter is also much greater, though this depends very much on the breed of dog in question. A general rule is the larger the breed of dog, the larger the number of puppies. The tiny Toy dogs often only have two or three in a litter, whereas a Great Dane is more likely to have nine or ten.

The biggest number of living puppies reared in one litter appears to be nineteen, born to a Great Dane bitch. Other breed records include Irish Setters and Doberman Pinschers with seventeen, Golden Retrievers with sixteen, and Border

These English Setters already have the freckles which add so much to their beauty. The long silky coat will appear when they are older.

Miniature Poodles at a particularly helpless stage before their eyes open.

Terrier puppies make hardy, fun-loving pets. They are usually full of curiosity and mischief.

Collies, Poodles, and Airedale Terriers with fifteen. Of course no bitch can rear such a number on her own and puppies in such large litters have to have extra feeds from a bottle right from birth. Six, or at the most eight, is about the number a bitch can rear comfortably without extra help, other than a very generous amount of food.

All puppies, whatever their breed, look very much the same at birth. They are blind and deaf and covered with short, sleek fur. Their muzzles are blunt and their ears are folded and crumpled. Their legs seem too small for their bodies and cannot yet support the puppy's weight. There are differences in birth weights between breeds of course, but these differences are not as great as might be expected. A puppy of a Toy breed might weigh four ounces at birth and grow up to be a six pound adult. To do this it would have to increase its body weight by twenty four times. A puppy of a much larger breed might well weigh two pounds when born and weigh a hundred pounds when adult. To do this its body weight increases fifty times, so even proportionally it has a lot more growing to do. This is one of the reasons that large breeds are slower to develop and mature.

The small dog may be fully grown by eight months but one of the giant breeds won't be mature until two and a half or three years of age. Because big dogs need extra food for growth for such a long time, they are even more expensive to keep than many people realise.

One of the hazards of buying a mongrel is that you can have little idea of the size and shape it will be when adult. There are some clues. A fluffy coated puppy will normally become a long-haired adult, and puppies whose feet appear too big for their size often grow into large dogs. With a purebred dog the rather nondescript shape of the newborn whelp changes very quickly as it begins to resemble its parents. The muzzle lengthens and the characteristic body shape of the breed begins to appear. The Greyhound or the Borzoi, both long-legged, elegant dogs built for speed, do not therefore have puppies which look like miniatures of themselves. Other changes during growth are even more startling, particularly in coat colour and length. All puppies are born with a short fine coat. By four to six weeks the ones who will become long-haired adults will present a fluffy appearance beside their smooth-coated brothers and sisters. This short, fluffy coat may not begin to change until the animal is six months old or more. When the adult coat comes through, it too may grow very slowly. Some breeds with profuse, long hair may take up to three years before their coat can be said to be fully grown.

Warm mother's milk gives the best start in life to all puppies, including Bull Terriers.

Though he may be the odd one out as regards colour, this Labrador pup gets more than his fair share of milk.

18

Colour, too, can change dramatically as an animal grows older. Kerry Blue Terriers, as their name suggests, are a dark, steel blue when adult. The puppies, however, are born black and may not become the proper colour until they are about a year old. Old English Sheepdog puppies are also born black with white markings and become grey when their adult coat appears.

Bedlington Terriers are another breed where the colour of the puppies is deceptive. As well as the more common blue, some Bedlingtons are liver-coloured, and these puppies are born a dark brown, only to fade to very pale fawn when they mature. The most dramatic change is in the Dalmatian, where the puppies are born completely white. The spots which give the breed its nickname of Plum Pudding dog, do not start to show through until the puppies are two or three weeks old.

Another difference in young dogs is in the carriage of the ears. Many breeds with upright ears, like Corgis or German Shepherd dogs, have lop-eared puppies. The ears gradually become upright between the ages of three to six months. Dingo puppies too have their ears folded over, though they stand up straight in the adult animal. All the wild dogs have prick ears. As they depend so much, when hunting, on an acute sense of hearing, this is obviously the most efficient shape. Man has bred many breeds with ears that hang down. It is difficult to prove that dogs like the Spaniel don't hear as well as their wild relatives because all dogs are so much better at hearing faint sounds than man himself! In some countries, breeds like Great Danes and Boxers have their ears cropped. In other words, the overhanging flap is cut off, leaving them with a small prick ear. This is done to improve their looks and give them a more alert and intelligent expression.

Though the hair is short, the dense, fluffy coat of the puppies indicates that they will finally grow the abundant, springy hair of their Rough Collie mother.

20

Large dogs tend to have large litters and this brindly Great Dane looks as though she finds hers a rather tiring responsibility.

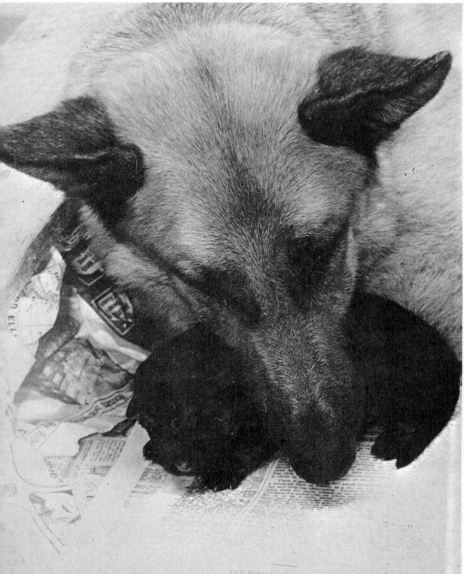

The Alsatian, or German Shepherd, is the most popular breed in the world. Though they look rather wolf-like, there is no proved connection between the two species.

Two things are vital for very young puppies and these are food and warmth. All animals have methods to keep their body temperature constant even though the temperature of their surroundings alters. We shiver when we are cold in order to raise our body temperature. In cold weather, birds fluff out their feathers so that a large amount of warm air is trapped close to their skin. When we are too hot we sweat and the evaporation of sweat on our skin helps to cool us. In the same circumstances the dog pants. For the first few days of their life puppies have not got this ability to keep themselves warm. In this state they are almost like reptiles whose body temperature varies according to the temperature of their surroundings. Puppies at this stage in their lives depend on keeping in contact with their mother to keep warm. The instinct of the bitch is to stay constantly with her new-born litter and very often she cannot be persuaded to leave them for more than a minute or two. Another advantage of having a box as a bed for the mother and puppies is that the mother's body heat, trapped in an

St. Bernards, too, are liable to have a lot of puppies. The cost of rearing several large dogs like these is often very heavy.

A litter of fifteen puppies is something of a record for this Old English Sheepdog. Although the puppies are born black and white, they will end up grey with white markings, like their mother.

enclosed space, helps to keep the puppies' surroundings warm. Some people like to use an infra-red lamp to heat the bed but this can have the disadvantage, particularly with long-haired breeds, of making the mother too hot and uncomfortable. Another method of keeping the puppies warm is to use some form of heating pad at the bottom of the box. However if you have a bed which is dry and draught free and is roofed in some way, the bitch herself will keep the puppies warm enough.

Puppies who cannot find their mother to snuggle close to, begin to whimper and cry and crawl round in circles. This distress cry is enough to bring their mother quickly back. If for some reason she is not there, the puppies' movements get slower and slower as they get colder and colder. In this state all their bodily functions get slower and slower too. Their heart does not beat as fast and they cannot digest any food they may be given, though their lives may still be saved by placing them in contact with heat, and feeding them when their movements get decidedly more vigorous.

As soon as a puppy is born, its mother gives it a thorough wash. This licking is often quite rough and it has the effect of warming and drying the puppy and helping it to start breathing. The puppy often begins to cry, which helps it to enlarge its lungs and breathe in more air. A puppy that appears lifeless when born can often be revived by rubbing it with a warm dry towel firmly enough to start the blood circulating faster and encourage breathing. As soon as the first clean up is over, the puppy will nose round until it finds one of its mother's teats and then start to feed. If you look inside the mouth of a very young puppy, you will see that the tongue, instead of being flat, is rather curved, almost like a scoop. This is a very efficient sucking mechanism. If you are bottle feeding a strong and healthy puppy and try to pull the teat out of its mouth before it has had enough, you will find it surprisingly difficult. When puppies are feeding, they also knead the mother's milk glands with their front paws. This paddling movement stimulates the flow of milk. Because they use their paws to increase the amount of milk they are getting, it is wise when the puppies are ten days old or so to snip off the tips of their claws, which are otherwise liable to scratch the mother and make her sore.

Both the tiny Chihuahua and the enormous St. Bernard spend quite a lot of time playing with their puppies. These games are great fun to watch and are obviously much enjoyed by everyone. Playing helps the puppies to grow stronger and more active. The adult Chihuahua, by the way, does not weigh very much more than a new born St. Bernard puppy.

The glamorous American Cocker Spaniel is slightly smaller and more heavily coated than its English relative.

Bitch's milk is much richer than cow's milk. It has more fat in it and more protein, the substances we need for growth. The first milk that the mother produces for her puppies is called colostrum. This contains even more fat, proteins and vitamins than the milk she has later. Even more important, it contains antibodies. These are substances which give the puppies protection for the first few weeks of their lives against certain diseases. They help to kill off some of the harmful bacteria, so the first few feeds are vital for the puppies' health.

Occasionally a bitch will push one particular puppy away and not allow it to feed. These rejected puppies may look identical to the rest of the litter but even if they are hand-reared they often prove to be weaklings and die early.

When the puppies are about three weeks old it is time to start weaning them by gradually introducing other foods into their diet as well as their mother's milk. The more smoothly and gradually this is done, the better. The first feeds should be of milk thickened with one of the baby cereals. The puppies have to be taught to lap and this is best done by gently pushing their muzzles into the mixture. Once they have discovered the taste by licking their lips they soon learn to take the milk from a

A pair of eight week old Pug puppies.

dish. Meat should be introduced a little later and has to be very finely minced or scraped. Their mother should be allowed to feed them when she wishes, but normally by the time they are six or seven weeks old she will only stay with them at night, and they should be having four or five meals spaced out during the day.

Wild dogs regurgitate food to wean their cubs. In other words they bring up partially digested food from their stomachs. Some pet dogs will do the same and, though it does not look very nice, it does no harm provided the bitch does not go short herself.

Puppies open their eyes about the tenth day. Likè kittens and most human babies their eyes are blue. This colour darkens until at eight or nine weeks old, the eyes are the colour they will be when the dog is adult. In many breeds eye colour is considered very important and usually dark eyes are preferred. This however is just fashion and the colour of the eye has nothing to do with how well a dog sees. A few dogs retain one or both blue eyes all their lives. This happens in the Siberian Husky and a number of the sheepdog breeds, where a blue eye is called a china or wall eye. Where a Sheepdog had odd eyes,

Many people think of Labrador Retrievers as always being black, but they can also be yellow — a colour which may vary from cream to fox-red — or an even rarer, liver-colour. Although the light puppy here looks as if it is the odd man out, it is a perfectly correct colour for a Labrador to be. These puppies are at the weaning stage. In other words they are learning to eat solid food instead of depending on their mother's milk. (Right)

Many orphan animals have been reared by bitches along-side their own puppies. This Terrier is feeding a young Puma kitten together with her own youngster.

the shepherd is supposed to have believed that the brown eye was for seeing sheep in the distance and the blue eye for seeing the flock close by. This story is not based on fact, however, and dogs with blue eyes have just as good sight as those with brown.

The first set of teeth, called the milk teeth, grow through the gums about the second or third week of life. By the fifth or sixth week the full set of these temporary teeth are through. There are twenty-eight of these and they are very white in colour and also very sharp. The permanent or adult teeth start to grow through and push out the baby teeth at three and a half to four months of age. There are usually forty-two of these and sometimes cutting these teeth may cause the puppy some pain and trouble. The puppy should be provided with plenty of things to chew as this helps to loosen the baby teeth. Occasionally the milk teeth do not get pushed out and it is wise to get a veterinary surgeon to remove them as they can cause the permanent teeth to grow crooked. Anything which is given to a puppy to chew must be too tough for the puppy to tear pieces off and swallow, as pieces of rubber, plastic or bone in the stomach can cause serious complications.

One of the Husky dogs that accompanied Wally Herbert's Trans-Arctic Expedition and her five puppies born in quarantine.

In breeds with pricked ears like these Corgis, the ears do not become erect until the dogs are between four to six months old.

In their behaviour bitches vary considerably when they have a litter. Some are quite happy to let their owners and friends look at and handle the puppies almost from birth. Others become very wild and resent anyone going near the youngsters when they are very young. Bitches of this type should have their desire for privacy respected and not be worried by visitors. Of course a watch has to be kept on the litter to make sure all is going well. Healthy contented puppies do not make a great deal of noise in the first weeks of life. Any prolonged and continuous crying means that something is wrong and is usually provoked by either hunger or cold. During the first three weeks or so the bitch keeps the puppies clean by licking them all over. This also encourages the puppies to have a bowel movement and pass out all the waste products from the body. The mother keeps the nest clean by clearing up the mess.

As soon as the puppies become active the bitch should have somewhere like a bench to jump on to, where she can get away from the youngsters if she wishes. Otherwise they will worry her continually. Working dogs like sheepdogs often leave their litters quite early on and get back to their work in the fields. They return at about four hourly intervals to feed the pups, but only remain with them at night.

Rearing orphan puppies is a full time job. With tiny breeds an obliging cat, who has just had kittens, can sometimes be persuaded to take on the job. Sometimes another bitch with a litter can be a foster mother. Her instinct will be to reject strange puppies, so they must be introduced when she is not there and allowed to mix with her own so that they have something of the same smell. Even then a close watch must be kept to see that she does not throw them out. If all else fails, the puppies can be bottle fed, using a doll's feeding bottle or premature baby's bottle. As we have seen, cow's milk is not rich enough and it is easiest to use a milk powder specially manufactured for feeding puppies. They need four hourly feeds throughout the day and night for the first week and must be kept very warm.

A dozen Great Danes is not an unusually large litter for a breed of this enormous size.

Six week-old Golden Labrador puppies suck greedily from their patient mother.

# PUPPY BEHAVIOUR

This six-week old Beagle puppy shows off her newly acquired skill.

As far as bones go — the bigger the better. Tackling the meaty end in this picture is a Bull Mastiff puppy.

The nearest wild relative to the dog, the Wolf, is a social animal. It lives in a pack with others of its own kind. Order in the pack is maintained by having a pack leader whom the others obey. This is usually the biggest and strongest male. As he grows older and weaker he will be replaced. As well as having a leader, the other Wolves in the pack have a social order, the weakest giving way to all the others while those in the middle defer to those above them in the social scale and take precedence over those below them. This system where each animal knows his place in relation to the others, prevents the pack being torn apart by needless fighting. Wolves do not have a vocal language to tell each other their intentions like we do. Instead they communicate with facial expressions and various tail movements.

Because the dog is a social animal like the Wolf it forms a much closer relationship with man than does the cat, which is more solitary in its habits. When you take a puppy into your home it is as if it had adopted your family as its pack. When a dog wags its tail you know that it is pleased, but if you also watch its face, and in particular the position of its ears, you can tell a lot more about its feelings. You can see whether it is frightened, or playful, or interested, or just simply bored.

Much of a dog's behaviour is learnt during puppyhood. For the first twenty-one days, the puppy's surroundings have little

These plates are being polished so thoroughly by these Cocker Spaniel puppies that washing them up will not be much of a problem.

Beagles, hounds with a long history, have only recently become popular as pets. Queen Elizabeth I, who was very fond of hunting, is known to have had a pack of pocket Beagles who were all under ten inches high. The height most favoured today is between thirteen and sixteen inches. Beagle packs hunt hares and are followed on foot. The smooth coat can be any colour except chocolate, and the gay angle of the tail gives a clue to the breed's merry and adventurous character. Because they have been bred as hunting dogs for so long some Beagles like to wander, and all Beagles need plenty of exercise.

The smart appearance of the Beagle makes it a great favourite. Bred for many centuries to hunt in packs, Beagles are independent animals, sometimes inclined to roam. In America they have been among the most popular of breeds for a number of years.

or no effect on it. Though the eyes are open earlier and the puppy can also hear, the brain and nervous system are not sufficiently developed for it to relate cause and effect. Though it can hear a bang it cannot relate it to a door closing, for example. The only thing it really responds to, except the presence of its mother, is heat or cold.

At three weeks old the brain works well enough for the puppy to be able to respond to the information it receives from its sense organs. In other words it is able to see, hear and smell. It is also beginning to move about, for its legs are now strong enough to support its body weight. Instead of crawling about the nest, it now learns to walk. The instinct to keep the nest clean is inborn and as soon as the puppy can walk it will move away from the sleeping area before relieving itself. This instinct to keep the place where it lives reasonably clean is the one we want to foster when we house-train a puppy. If puppies are brought up in a very small space which they cannot avoid getting dirty, they are much harder to house-train later on. At this stage the mother stops clearing up after the litter.

The puppies begin to bark and to attempt to play with each other and with their mother. They start to explore and take an interest in their surroundings, though they do not yet go very far from their bed. This period of play is important for a number of reasons. It strengthens the puppies' muscles. In wild dogs many of the movements they make in fun will be the movements they will later make in earnest when catching and

Golden Retriever pups are among the most appealing of breeds.

killing their prey. Mock fighting takes place among the members of the litter and this establishes which puppy will be the leader of the group. This struggle to be top dog begins even earlier, when the biggest and most determined puppies feed from the teats at the back of their mother, where they are kept warmer under her thigh and where the milk supply is more abundant. Normally the biggest male tends to become the leader, just as in a wild pack. In a litter of bitch puppies, it is often the noisiest female who occupies the position. The mother disciplines the litter, growling and snarling if they pester her unduly or are too rough in their play. This, also, is very important for the puppies' development and there is evidence that if, for any reason, a puppy misses this period of play with its litter mates and its mother, it may never have a normal relationship with other dogs when it is adult. It may, in fact, become a life-long bully or coward.

A Boxer puppy will end up measuring about twenty-two inches at the shoulder and weighing around sixty-five pounds. This breed originally came from Germany where they are still used as guard and police dogs. They make cheerful, alert and energetic pets.

The British Bulldog presents a four-square appearance to the world. (Right)

Toy Poodles are some of the best sellers in the dog world.

By the time they are three months, puppies are very adventurous and investigate everything that comes their way. At this age they won't go very far from their owner when they are in strange surroundings, but unless this early habit is reinforced by training, you may find your young dog quite happy to wander off on his own as he gets bigger and bolder. Healthy young dogs have boundless energy and need plenty of food, both to keep them going and to provide for growth. Most breeds from the age of six months until they are mature need something like one and a half times the amount of food needed to feed a fully grown and rather more sedate adult. They also need plenty of games with their owners or other dogs, and some form of training if they are to become well-mannered. Bored dogs, that have little to look forward to except the next meal, will sometimes turn their energies to rather destructive uses.

Full of life and energy, a Miniature Poodle puppy shows how good it is to be alive. The adult Poodle coat is just beginning to grow through at four months old. At this age it is wise to introduce the puppy to the clippers so that he can gradually become used to the idea of being clipped and trimmed.

Cocker Spaniel puppies are well-known for their playfulness.

One small cuddly animal becomes ....

. . . this large and mournful dog later on. The name Bloodhound suggests a dog of the utmost ferocity but in fact most Bloodhounds are rather gentle, melancholy dogs and the name probably first meant pure-blooded or aristocratic.

By way of contrast, here is the smallest breed of dog in the world, the Chihuahua. Some of these can weigh as little as two pounds, and are really too small to stand up to the rough and tumble of family life.

# CHOOSING A PUPPY

As you can see from the pictures in this book, all puppies have a great deal of charm and sometimes choosing one can be a little too easy. As we have seen, dogs need companionship and it is kinder to choose some less demanding pet if your dog will have to be shut up by itself nearly all day and every day. All dogs need exercise and someone has to be responsible for giving the dog at least one daily walk, whatever the weather. A dog, to remain healthy, must be well fed and some of the giant breeds are very expensive to rear. Even the more popular medium sized breeds can place quite a strain on the family budget. All dogs need regular grooming but with the long-haired breeds this is a daily necessity. The glamour of the Afghan Hound, or the shaggy appeal of the Old English Sheepdog, depends very much on the time and trouble taken by their owners.

Most puppies are sold when they are about eight weeks old and the first essential is to pick your puppy from a healthy litter. Healthy puppies have loose, supple skins and clear, bright eyes. When they are awake they are interested in their surroundings and should not be listless. If you can see their mother and father, so much the better, for this will tell you a little about the temperament and character that the puppies are likely to have. Bitches who have just reared a litter often look a little unkempt, but they should not appear half-starved, as this might well indicate that the puppies also have not had a good start in life. Try to pick a bold and friendly puppy, as youngsters that seem nervous in familiar surroundings will be doubly so in strange ones. Finally it is always possible to get a veterinary opinion as to the health or otherwise of the puppy you are thinking of purchasing.

There are over three hundred different breeds of dog in the world, so even leaving out all the rarities and oddities, it is only possible to mention comparatively few in a book like this.

Sealyham Terriers, like this one, were originally bred to kill vermin which included anything from badgers and polecats to rats. Their short legs enabled them to go underground after their quarry and they had to have immense courage for their size. Nowadays they are all kept as pets and this appealing puppy demonstrates their breed's charm. Many Sealyhams are comical characters who delight in making their owners laugh at their antics.

There are many books which list every available breed but it is better still to go to a large dog show and have a look round. You may find that the breed you fancy has an irritating bark, or looks quite different in the flesh, or is even unobtainable.

Breeds of dogs fall roughly into groups. The Mastiff group includes many of the giants of the dog world, as well as those with flattened or foreshortened muzzles like the Bulldog. Great Danes are probably the best known of the really large breeds. Their history includes being used for hunting wild boar and adorning the courts of the German aristocracy. Because of their size and strength they need to be properly trained. Two others of the big breeds, the Newfoundland and the St. Bernard, are well known because of their reputation for saving lives. The Newfoundland is a strong swimmer and was originally a fisherman's dog, helping to haul in the nets and rescue anything that went overboard. The St. Bernard helped the monks of St. Bernard guide travellers through snowy mountain passes in the Alps. Both of these breeds are now gentle, rather lumbering beasts of great weight and substance. The most popular among the Mastiff type dogs is probably the Boxer. This is a medium sized, powerful dog, used on the continent for police work, but better known in Britain and the U.S.A. as a companion and pet. They are alert and boisterous dogs which make good guards of family property. The Boston Terrier, America's national breed, is one of the smallest members of this group. The clearly defined markings of white on the black, or dark brindle, coat give it a very smart appearance. It should weigh less than twenty-five pounds and is a faithful and affectionate little dog. The French Bulldog is another small breed with a wrinkled face and immense charm.

A young Saluki.

Italian Greyhound puppies look relatively undistinguished compared with their elegant, fine-boned mother. Tiny, graceful, high-stepping dogs, these are the Toy version of a racing Greyhound.

The Hounds can also be divided into two groups—those that hunt by scent and those that hunt by sight. The latter are sometimes called Gazehounds and include one of the most elegant as well as the fastest of all the breeds, the Greyhound. Greyhounds are usually kept for racing and their smaller relation, the Whippet, is more often kept as a pet and companion. A Greyhound from the Middle East is the Saluki, a dog kept by the desert sheiks to hunt gazelle. The Borzoi, or Russian Wolfhound, had an equally aristocratic background, being kept by Russian noblemen for hunting Wolves. The Afghan hound is another member of this group of dogs built for speed. Many of these breeds have a long and ancient history, for Greyhound type dogs are found in carvings and paintings dating back to 3000 B.C.

The Terriers are the noisy, excitable extroverts of the dog world. They are often hardy, fun-loving individuals full of energy and bounce. Most of these breeds are British in origin and they range in size from the Airedale, which measures twenty-four inches at the shoulder, down to the Norwich, which is only eleven inches high. Most were bred in the past for ratting or bolting foxes and badgers from their lairs.

The black and tan Airedale is nicknamed the King of Terriers. This dog is easy to teach and has been used for many purposes, from police work to finding people buried under rubble after bombing raids. Other long-legged Terriers with harsh coats include the Lakeland, the Welsh and the Irish. Also from Ireland comes the Kerry Blue Terrier with a soft, abundant wavy coat. Both these Irish breeds are sweet tempered with their owners but inclined to resent other dogs. Smooth coated Terriers include the Bull Terrier, the gladiator of the canine race. This dog combines a powerful appearance with a jaunty air and possesses both courage and loyalty. The Manchester

49

Terrier is also smooth coated and is a graceful black and tan dog of about sixteen inches. The Bedlington is the one that looks like a lamb. This Terrier was once the companion of tinkers in the Border country between England and Scotland. They used it for killing vermin on weekdays and for racing on Sundays. The Fox Terrier can be either wire-haired or smooth and in the 1920s was one of the most popular of breeds. Nearly all the wire-haired Terriers mentioned need trimming if they are to have a look of smartness. The short-legged terrier breeds come mainly from Scotland and include the Cairn, the Dandie Dinmont, the Scottish and the West Highland White Terrier. Though these dogs may be smaller in stature they are just as bold and energetic as their larger brothers.

One of the breeds that has rocketed to popularity in recent years is the Poodle. Poodles come in three sizes, although the largest size, the Standard, has rather been left out in the cold compared with the Miniature and the Toy. A profuse coat, which needs a good deal of clipping, is a relic of the days when the breed was used for retrieving water-fowl and ducks. Poodles come in solid colours and are lively and intelligent.

One of the earliest uses that man found for the dog was to control his flocks and herds. Perhaps because they have been in such close association with men for so long, the Sheepdogs are among the most easily trained and responsive of dogs. Many of these breeds no longer do their original job but have the equally responsible one of being the family friend and companion. The ones who still work sheep are the Border Collies. These are lithe, clever and energetic animals with an inborn desire to work. Because of this they do not always make good pets, becoming highly strung and moody when kept inactive.

The Rough Collie with its profuse coat is a splendid animal. The coat can be sable, blue merle, or black and tan with white

markings and there should be a well developed mane and frill setting off the narrow, aristocratic-looking head. The Shetland Sheepdog looks like a Rough Collie in miniature. They are a gentle, affectionate breed of convenient size and attractive to look at. The Old English Sheepdog is a large, shaggy beast with a lot of clumsy charm. They are a good deal more active than their bear-like exterior might suggest, but they do need a great deal of grooming. Among the smaller herding dogs we find the two kinds of Welsh Corgi who were used for droving cattle. The Pembrokeshire Corgi with the docked tail is by far the best known. Like many cattle dogs, it has a loud bark for its size which is very effective in keeping out intruders. The Alsatian, or German Shepherd, is perhaps the most versatile and best known of this group of dogs. Used the world over as police dogs, army dogs and guides for the blind, they are also trusted and valued members of many families.

The Hounds that hunt by following the scent of their quarry are not as fast moving as the Greyhound type. Their job is to wear down their victims by keeping on their trail rather than catching their prey by sheer speed. Greyhounds run silently, needing all their breath for galloping. Hounds that follow a scent yelp and whimper with excitement. This hound 'music' tells the huntsman how far ahead and in which direction the quarry is moving. One of this type of hound, the Beagle, has been widely kept as a pet. The Beagle is a gay and independent character with a smart appearance and of a convenient size for the modern home. Having been kept for many generations in packs, Hounds are not usually quarrelsome, but they are very determined, a useful trait when following a cold and difficult scent. All these Hounds have long, hanging ears, but none more so than the Bloodhound, the most famed of tracking dogs, and its shorter-legged relative the Basset Hound. The

A Miniature Smooth Dachshund puppy looks at the world through incredibly appealing eyes.

looks of the latter are rather deceptive. It is really quite a large dog set on rather short legs. The Dachshund is another of the short-legged Hounds. Bred in the past for following badgers to ground, many Dachshunds still retain their sporting instincts.

The Spitz group of dogs all have prick ears, thick, stand-off coats and tails curled over their backs. The sledge dogs of the north come into this group as does the Norwegian Elkhound, the Keeshond, and the dwarf of the group, the Pomeranian. These are all lively dogs, alert, friendly towards people and fond of barking. The Chow Chow is rather the odd man out, being a reserved, self-reliant dog. Devoted to its owner, the Chow is too dignified to welcome the attention of strangers. The only tailless member of this group is the Schipperke. The name of this small, glossy black dog means 'little skipper' for the breed used to be watchdogs on the Belgian barges.

Though they look like genial Teddy bears, Chow Chows are usually one-man dogs, aloof with strangers.

The Toy group of dogs contains many breeds that are miniatures of the types of dog we have discussed previously. Many of these little dogs are tougher than they look and are ready to accompany their owners everywhere they want to go. Obviously though, care must be taken, since the consequences of accidentally treading on a Chihuahua are liable to be a good deal more serious for the dog than doing the same thing to a Great Dane.

A number of Toy breeds are believed to have come originally from the Far East. Among these are the Pekinese, the Japanese Spaniel and the Pug. The Pekinese has a romantic history, being bred for many centuries in the Imperial Palace at Pekin as an exclusively royal dog. Only when the Summer Palace in Pekin was ransacked by British soldiers in 1869 were five of these dogs brought back to the Western world. A handful more were smuggled out at the end of the nineteenth century and all the Pekinese today stem from this small nucleus. The Pug, too, enjoyed royal favour in Holland in the sixteenth century, and King Charles II of England kept a number of Toy Spaniels like the Cavalier King Charles of today. The tiniest of the Greyhounds, the Italian Greyhound, appears in many Tudor and Stuart portraits, and both the Maltese Terrier and the Papillon have histories showing that they have long been favourites with the court ladies. By contrast, the diminutive Brussels Griffon was kept by the cab-drivers of Brussels to keep down the rats in the stables, and the Yorkshire Terrier also started life as a ratter, being bred for the job by the miners in the north of England. Mention must also be made of a Tibetan breed, the Shih Tzu. Although its owners deny that it is a Toy dog, this active and arrogant little dog weighs considerably less than sixteen pounds.

The young Pekinese in the basket already has the commanding air of a born aristocrat, while the adult looks like someone who expects and appreciates only the best in life. This exotic, oriental Toy dog was not known to the Western world until the turn of this century, and then rapidly became the most popular of the Toy breeds, only recently being ousted by the Yorkshire Terrier. The boldness, self-esteem and individuality of these little lion dogs have captivated many people to whom the care such long coats demand is but a small price to pay for the pleasure of owning dogs of such character.

Some of the Gundog breeds are also deservedly popular as family dogs. In particular, the Labrador Retriever has many roles other than that of accompanying the sportsman. These dogs are used by the police and are frequently trained as guide dogs for the blind. There are four Retriever breeds of which the Labrador and the Golden Retriever are the two best known and loved. The work these dogs were originally bred for was to find and bring back the game that the sportsman shot.

Also well known in the Gundog group are the Spaniels. These are mentioned as far back as the sixteenth century by authors writing about dogs. They work by finding the game and flushing it from its hiding place, as well as bringing it back to hand when it has been shot. There are ten breeds of Spaniel known in Britain and America, but some of them are extremely rare. The Cocker Spaniel, both American and English, is by far the most numerous breed. They are merry little dogs whose tails never seem to stop wagging. Part of their charm lies in the variety of coat colours that are available, the speckled, or roan ones, being particularly attractive. The working ability has been lost in most of the dogs who are kept as pets only. The Springer Spaniel is rather larger, weighing nearly twice as much as the Cocker. These liver and white, or black and white, animals were used in the Middle Ages to find and spring birds into nets, and today many still work as gundogs.

The Setter breeds are dogs of great beauty with flat, silky coats. The Irish Setter is a rich chestnut and the rarer Gordon Setter is black and tan. The English Setter is freckled white.

Healthy puppies like these Pharaohs above have a well rounded appearance with loose supple skin and clear, bright eyes.

Good-natured and sensible, the Golden Retrievers on the right make excellent family dogs.

The soft appealing eyes of the Dandie Dinmont Terrier on the far right belie the determined independence of the breed.

# HOW TO LOOK AFTER YOUR PUPPY

An eight week old puppy is still very much a baby, and like all babies needs plenty of sleep and frequent feeds. Most people selling puppies will provide a diet sheet, giving details of food the puppy has been used to, but if this is missing remember that an eight week old baby should be having four meals a day. The quantity must be gradually increased as the pup grows, and the number of meals can be reduced to three a day when the animal is three months old, and to two a day when it is six months of age. An adult dog only needs one meal daily, though many owners still like to give an early morning biscuit or two. Two of those first puppy meals should be meat ones, and the other two must be milk with puppy meal, or biscuit. During the period of growth it is also wise to add some form of extra calcium to the diet and if the foods you are using have not already had it added, a little vitamin D in the form of cod liver oil. Because dogs vary in size so much, it is impossible to give much guidance as to the quantity of food. Many puppies will walk away from a dish when they have had enough, but some individuals are so greedy they will eat to bursting point.

The puppy should have a warm, dry, draught-proof bed of its own to retire to when it wants to rest. A cardboard box is a good bed at this stage as it can be thrown away when the puppy outgrows it or chews it to pieces. The bedding should be washable and the puppy should have some toys of its own that it can chew without coming to any harm. A large marrow bone will give a dog hours of enjoyment. Smaller bones that may splinter should be avoided, and poultry, rabbit and fish bones must never be given. Many toys are specially made and sold for dogs and it is up to you to choose one that cannot be taken apart and swallowed by the animal.

Young puppies get all the exercise they need in play and do not need regular long walks until they are five or six months old. They should be taken about before this to help them get used to meeting people and noisy traffic, but do not let them get too tired. Teaching a dog to walk on a collar and lead can be

A safe, comfortable way to hold a dog.

started in the house. A lightweight puppy collar should be buckled loosely round the puppy's neck and left on until the dog does not notice it any more. When you clip the lead on persuade the puppy to come a few steps with you and praise it as soon as it does. Short, pleasant lessons at regular intervals are much better than the occasional long struggle. Coaxing a puppy or bribing it with a titbit will help persuade it that going for a walk on a collar and lead is a pleasure. When your dog gets enthusiastic, you may have the opposite trouble and find you are being pulled along. This should be stopped with a sharp jerk on the lead and the word 'No'. Only give praise when the dog is walking quietly by your side.

Puppies will learn to come to their names quite quickly if they are always called to something pleasant like food or a game.

Each. dog is an individual with a different character and different ways of reacting and behaving. All of them, however, will repay your time and trouble with a devotion that no other animal has ever given to man.

A Boxer puppy.

Patient training helps in the show ring.

## ACKNOWLEDGEMENTS

Animal Photography 14, 18, 20, 24, 38, 41, 43T, 43B, 44, 49, 61; Barnaby's Picture Library 25; Mary Eleanor Browning 13, 40B, 45; Central Press Photos Ltd 10; Camera Press 27, 28, 55; C. M. Cooke & Son 50; Will Green 37B; Nelson Groffman 57BL; Vanessa Hamilton 33; The Hamlyn Group 22, 60; Keystone Press Agency 12, 16T, 31, 37T, 40T; Paul Popper Ltd 7, 36, 46, 47, 52; Photo Researchers 8T, 8B, 9, 11, 15; Pictorial Press 21T, 21B, 26, 32, 39, 48, 51, 53, 56–57T; Rex Features 54, 57BR; Michael Starkey 59R; Michael Starkey and Tiopepi Dog Centre 16B, 58; Syndication International 23, 35, 59; Sally Anne Thompson 30, endpapers; John Topham Ltd 19, 29, 34, 42; Thomas A. Wilkie 53.

Cover, Keystone Press Agency; Frontispiece, Camera Press.